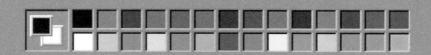

OF MOUSE AND MAN

The Best of Jim'll Paint It

unbound

This edition first published in 2019

Unbound
6th Floor Mutual House, 70 Conduit Street, London W1S 2GF

www.unbound.com

Text Design by Virtual 15

A CIP record for this book is available from the British Library

ISBN 978-1-78352-840-0 (trade hardback)
ISBN 978-1-78352-841-7 (ebook)

Printed in Slovenia by DZS Grafik

1 2 3 4 5 6 7 8 9

For everyone who asked me
to paint something for them.
Thank you for everything.

'You name it. I'll paint it. On Paint.'

It occurred to me recently that Jim'll Paint It is a product of impatience. It began life as a means of scratching a creative itch within a very short time frame – specifically, my half-hour lunch break. Why waste precious minutes thinking of what to draw when I could ask people for requests first thing in the morning and have a dozen or so ideas waiting should the opportunity for doodling arise? Why spend valuable seconds toying with Photoshop's dizzying array of tools with the alluring simplicity of Microsoft Paint just a click away? If Photoshop is the digital equivalent of an easel-mounted canvas and a shelf of expensive paints and brushes, then Paint has the immediacy of a Post-it note and a ballpoint pen.

My early efforts in Paint show this distinction quite clearly. They were crude, jagged and coloured with the lurid tones of the preset palette. But, almost immediately, the temptation to push the medium beyond its intended limits proved too strong for my obsessive nature to resist. Ironically, that which grew from restlessness soon became extraordinarily time-consuming as more detail was added with each subsequent piece. Half an hour of rough, freehand drawing became days of meticulous, pixel-by-pixel composition on ever larger canvases. As the paintings grew, so did their reach. There was no longer any need to ask my friends for ideas as I was being sent hundreds of them every week via social media in a beautiful 'you hum it and I'll play it' artist/audience dynamic, one which would have been completely unimaginable just ten years earlier. Thanks to this unique relationship, and with the support of people buying prints and T-shirts, I was able to quit my job and paint full time.

Since then I've finished just shy of 400 images. I've moved house twice in that time, and I can remember clearly which were the first pictures painted in each new home just as I can recall what music or audiobook I was listening to during the creation of a given piece. Some have particular memories attached to them, of good times and bad. But I don't think there is a single one where I didn't, for a few hours, lose myself in that happy place. The one I was in such a mad rush to get to when I started all this. I feel blessed to visit that place nearly every day and proud to present this collection of the peculiar images I've found there.

Bottom vs Legion of Doom

5 October 2017
Requested by Michael Walsh

'Richie and Eddie from *Bottom* decide to take their slapstick fighting mainstream and become a tag team in early nineties WWF. Their first match is against the Legion of Doom. Their wrestling gear is simply their crusty underpants. Richie is receiving the Doomsday Device whilst Eddie is distracted getting drunk in the corner with Spudgun and Dave Hedgehog.'

Dad's Army of Darkness

24 August 2017
Requested by GeekCliche (via Twitter)

Star Trek: The Next Generation Game

17 August 2017
Requested by Martyn Huyton-Berry

Home Improvement Blobby

4 May 2017

Requested by Alex and Phil

'Dear Jim,
Please could you paint a picture of Mr Blobby decorating his new house with his new family using Noel Edmonds' skin as wallpaper and his bones as ornaments while their new pet Jack Whitehall is in a huge puppy crate looking frightened for his life as Baby Blobby is grinning at him.'

With acknowledgement to Charlie Adams, creator of Mr Blobby

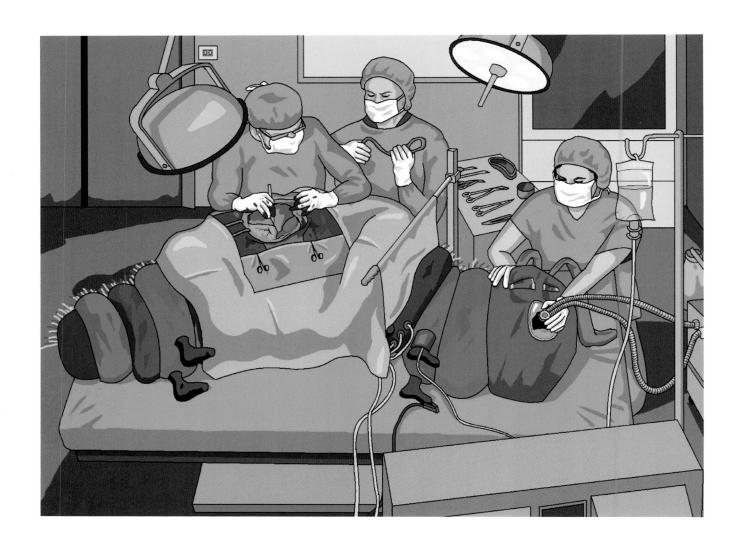

Gastric Surgery

21 August 2014
Requested by Si

'Dear Jim,
Can you paint the very hungry caterpillar undergoing gastric bypass surgery?'

Kitty Feltz Rides Godzilla

26 August 2015
Requested by Roo James

'Vanessa Feltz dressed as Hello Kitty, riding Godzilla through the streets of Tokyo as Bruce Willis leads a small army of clowns in an attempt to take her down.'

Vanessa Feltz liked this image so much that, according to her producer at Radio 2, she bought every copy of the card on which it was featured from the Paperchase near the studio.

Chefs

Like the photorealists your sixth form art teacher probably scorned, I have always enjoyed the physical process of creation more than the mental process of conception. In a world brimming with untamed visual creativity from every walk of life, what would I – a middle-class white male – be bringing to the table in terms of meaningful conceptual artwork anyway? Far better, I thought, to use my obsessive urge to create as a conduit for those with ideas but no ability or inclination to render them visually. So, I asked the world what it would like to see… and the world said it would like to see British celebrity chefs.

In the first month of the project's existence I was asked to paint Loyd Grossman being angry about ravioli, Heston Blumenthal playing Connect 4 with a dinosaur, Antony Worrall Thompson stealing a fish tank, Gregg Wallace and John Torode judging Pinhead on *MasterChef*, Nigella Lawson eating a bowl of Pentium 4 processors and Hugh Fearnley-Whittingstall on fire. So, of course, I painted them all.

To celebrate the fifth birthday of Jim'll Paint It – marking the day I first set up the Tumblr page – I decided to revisit one of my better-known chef-based paints: *Ainsley Harriott, Son of God*. The original was born from a short-lived 'five words or less' request challenge that also spawned *Tim Henman's Lovecraftian Bobsleigh Nightmare* and *Jeremy Clarkson Can't Eat Cereal*. Rather than just update the drawing style as I had done with the *Blessed vs Goldie Redux* (*page 25*), I decided to use it as a chance to add yet more celebrity chefs in the form of Ainsley's disciples.

Ainsley Harriott: Son of God Redux

21 February 2018
Requested by Stephen Savage Savage Savage

Carpathian Kitten Loss

9 March 2017
Requested by Chris Keane

'Peter Venkman releasing the ghost of Bob Ross to help Vigo's painting overcome his Carpathian kitten loss.'

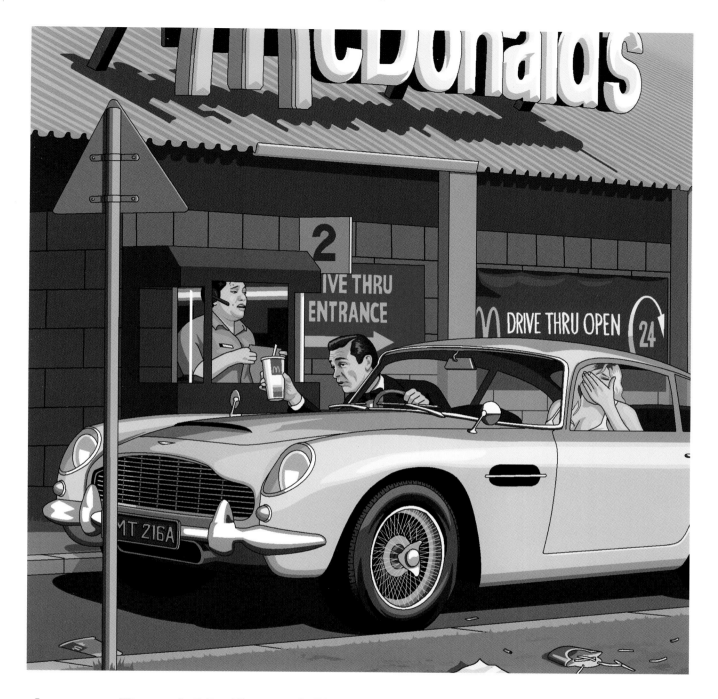

James Bond McDonald's Drive-thru

18 May 2017
Requested by Chris Milburn

'James Bond in his Aston Martin furtively ordering twenty Chicken McNuggets and a chocolate milkshake (shaken not stirred) from a McDonald's drive-thru.'

Elf Execution

12 October 2016
Requested by John Beacroft-Mitchell

'Dear Jim,
Could you please paint a picture of Father Christmas
reluctantly executing an elf over a trench of dead
elves because someone mentioned Christmas
before advent?'

Edmonds' Troubled Period

27 September 2016
Requested by Charlie Ray

'Dear Jim,
Can you please paint Noel Edmonds calling a cat to comfort him but the cat has turned the tables and ends up helping Noel get through what is clearly a very troubled period in his life?'

The Texas Chainsaw Manicure

5 March 2015
Requested by Ryan Marks

Normal Frasier

16 September 2015
Requested by James Grimley

'Dear Jim,
Please paint me a normal episode of *Frasier* except Niles is wearing a jetpack and using it to hover slightly and Frasier's forehead has become so grotesquely large it's started to absorb the apartment and everything in it. Martin is sitting in his chair like normal except he doesn't have any bones. There are severed heads strewn around and everything is on fire. Also the view of the Seattle skyline has been replaced by that of the Tower of Babel. Daphne is being stolen by ants.'

Festive Robin

24 November 2016
Requested by Lewis Goram

'Dear Jim,
Please could you paint me a festive scene
comprising a sixties Batman's tiny Robin shivering
on a snow-covered branch; in the background the
AA are giving the batmobile a jump-start.'

Chuckle Brothers Explore Aperture

30 December 2014
Requested by Sam Butterfield

'Dear Jim,
Can you paint me the Chuckle Brothers exploring
the Aperture Science testing facility?'

Hoover Racing

The idea of repainting one of my rough, early pieces had been knocking around my head for a while. I was fast approaching half a million Facebook followers and decided I would celebrate by repainting Brian Blessed and Goldie racing each other on vacuum cleaners – an image that has become synonymous with Jim'll Paint It. In one of the proudest moments of my career, the legendary Brian Blessed himself reposted the original piece with the comment, 'Oh I think I could take Goldie, don't you? The Henry is a far superior vehicle to the Dyson when it comes to White Ace-fuelled karting.' At one point Goldie's son, Danny Price, sent in his own request: 'I'm Goldie's son Danny and for the last month or so every fucker in my town has come up to me asking, "Have you seen that picture of your dad riding a hoover?" So can you please draw a picture of me looking disappointed at the picture you drew of my dad whilst everyone around me points and laughs?'

I was a bit apprehensive about doing a George Lucas and 'improving' an early work, completely oblivious to the naive charm that actually made it good in the first place. Then I thought, 'Get over yourself, Jim. Your stupid doodle of Brian Blessed riding a Henry hoover isn't *Star Wars*.'

It turned out to be a fairly interesting exercise in seeing how much you can technically improve at something if you practise nearly every day for three years. The resulting image fits in much better with the rest of my work but I totally understand if people prefer the original. It's never my intention for a repaint to 'replace' an original.

Blessed vs Goldie Redux

4 March 2016
Requested by Tommy

'Dear Jim,
Please paint me a picture of Brian Blessed riding a
Henry hoover alongside D'n'B DJ Goldie on a Dyson.
They are racing on the *Mario Kart* level Rainbow Road
and are both drunk on White Ace cider.'

The Photo Challenges

In the summer of 2014 I ran a photo competition in which followers could recreate their favourite Jim'll Paint It pictures in real life. The victory prize was a painting of anything the winner wished. The effort involved in some of the entries was truly humbling, none more so than that of Eirah Lewis, Adam Young and Matt Young, who ambitiously took on one of my abstract early works, earning them a portrait of the three of them battling a cosmic octopus *(see page 28).*

In 2017 I ran the competition again and the entries were even more impressive. Perhaps the most uncanny of all was the astonishingly accurate depiction of Blessed and Goldie racing on vacuum cleaners created by Katie and Dave and photographed by their friend Andy.

As is always the case when I offer to paint *anything* as a prize, I was a little concerned they would come back with an extensive, everything-but-the-kitchen-sink brief. Sure enough, that's exactly what they sent. And who can blame them, really? The premise was simple enough but the list of required details made it possibly the most complex request I've ever taken on. It was slow going but I was determined not to balk, keeping in mind the effort they'd put into their photo and how lovely, genuine and enthusiastic they were in correspondence.

Katie and Dave are both doctors so I included the Jeremy Hunt hide rug as a bonus prize.

Teds' Revenge

4 September 2018

Requested by Katie, Dave and Andy

'Picture the inside of a hunting lodge: wooden walls, big majestic fireplace with roaring fire and huge boardroom table with high-backed chairs. This is the Annual Ted Revenge Meeting. SuperTed is chairing the meeting and pointing at a flipchart headed 'Most wanTED'. On it are all the pictures of the people they're hunting and want revenge on. All the famous teds are sat round the table at the meeting... Bungle, Rupert, Sooty, etc. but other Teds clearly feel left out and want to be involved, so they've come in disguise. Father Ted is sat there wearing some rubbish bear ears and a nose and wants revenge on Bishop Brennan and Ted from 'Bill & Ted' has just arrived in his phonebox. Me and Dave have snuck in wearing really lame bear disguises and are worried we are going to be rumbled any minute!'

Please note this is a heavily abbreviated version of the original request which included most of the details in the image.

Battling the Cosmic Octopus

11 September 2014
Requested by Eirah Lewis, Adam Young and Matt Young

'The three of us battling the Psychedelic Cosmic Octopus (badly) while God (played by Gazza) tries to rescue us with a fishing rod and chicken. Meanwhile in the foreground a greyhound dressed like Charles Dickens licks the frosting off some doughnuts.'

This was the prize portrait for the winners of the 2014 Photo Challenge (see previous page).

Jedi Flashheart

14 June 2018
Requested by Tomos Martin

'In honour of the anniversary of Rik Mayall's passing and Ade Edmondson being in *The Last Jedi*, I'd love it if you painted Flashheart as a Jedi master posing suggestively with a fully lit lightsaber while women of various species swoon over him. In the background Darth Vyvyan is beating Jar Jar Binks with a frying pan.'

North Korean Teletubbies

23 April 2015
Requested by Lee Bryant

'Dear Jim,
As they're due to be making a return this year, can
you paint it for me to see what the *Teletubbies* might
look like were it to be broadcast in North Korea?'

With acknowledgement to Anne Wood and Andrew Davenport, creators of the Teletubbies

Speed Awareness Course

4 September 2014
Requested by Krispie McBride

'Crash Bandicoot at a speed awareness course with
other *Mario Kart* and *Wacky Races* characters.'

With acknowledgement to William Hanna and Joseph Barbera, creators of *Wacky Races*; and Shigeru Miyamoto, creator of *Super Mario Kart*

E17 8ET

8 November 2018
Requested by Peter Brennan

'Dear Jim,
My postcode is E17 8ET, which, as the guy at the Oyster card complaints department pointed out recently, sounds like Walthamstow's own classic pop band chomping down on Steven Spielberg's stumpy-legged alien. I'd love to have that image rendered in paint form and available in a format I could hang on my living-room wall. That way no one would ever again need ask me my postcode when drunkenly ordering food online. Cheers!'

Mugabe McDonald's Coup

28 November 2017
Requested by Graham Moore

'Can you paint Robert Mugabe working at
McDonald's please? He's doing such a poor job of
running the place that item costs are in the trillions
of Zimbabwean dollars, and the regular staff (Ronald
McDonald, Grimace, etc.) have launched a coup.'

Pilkington Dobby

26 July 2016
Requested by Adam Birkett

'Dear Jim,
Can you please draw Stephen Merchant giving Karl
Pilkington a sock and freeing him from the clutches
of Ricky Gervais.'

Spider-Man Whiplash

16 February 2017
Requested by Dominic Burchnall

'Dear Jim,
Could you paint Spider-Man sitting at a drum kit
bawling his eyes out, while J. K. Simmons in full J.
Jonah Jameson costume pelts him with Uncle Ben's
rice and yells at him to stay in time?'

Wacky Racists

7 June 2018
Requested by Bangor Spruytenberg

A Swan Wearing Björk as a Dress

29 March 2019

Requested by Kirsty Phipps

Zucked

On 16 October 2016 I logged on to my Facebook page to check for new requests to paint in the coming week. To my abject horror all of my visitor posts had mysteriously vanished. I was suddenly all too aware of how much my livelihood depends on both the amazing requests I get sent on a daily basis and the arbitrary whims of Facebook. In a panic I created a post explaining what had happened and asked for people to reply with any requests they might have.

My favourite of these was Niall Graham's theory as to what had happened to my visitor posts. Thankfully, a few days later they returned just as inexplicably as they had disappeared. Perhaps Zuck had a change of heart. Eagle-eyed readers may have already noticed the tape over the webcam – a precaution that the real Zuckerberg is known to take. Also, the world map in the background was, at the time, an accurate depiction of countries in which Facebook was the most used social media website.

Zuckerberg World Domination

20 October 2016
Requested by Niall Graham

'Please paint your CEO man Mark from Facebook deleting all the lovely requests for your paintings. With a menacing look on his face. And possibly an evil laugh. Maybe also in the back a map showing his plan for world domination. Maybe show a few photos on the walls of his rivals with knives thrown into them or something. And his stacks of money. Be creative.'

Hijack

14 August 2014
Requested by Jane Sayer

'Dear Jim,
Could you paint Rosie and Jim on the old *Ragdoll*
being hijacked by Somali pirates?'

Kim Jong-il: Spice Girls Fan

2 June 2014
Requested by Dave PGD

'Dear Jim,
The late Kim Jong-il was a massive fan of both the Spice Girls and fancy dress. Could you paint me a collage of Polaroids he took dressed up as every member standing in front of a giant letter such that it spells the word "Spice". Note he hasn't taken his glasses off for any of the pictures and when dressed as Ginger Spice he is wearing a North Korean flag dress instead of the Union Jack dress. He has also included magazine cut-outs saying "girl power" and "spice up your life".'

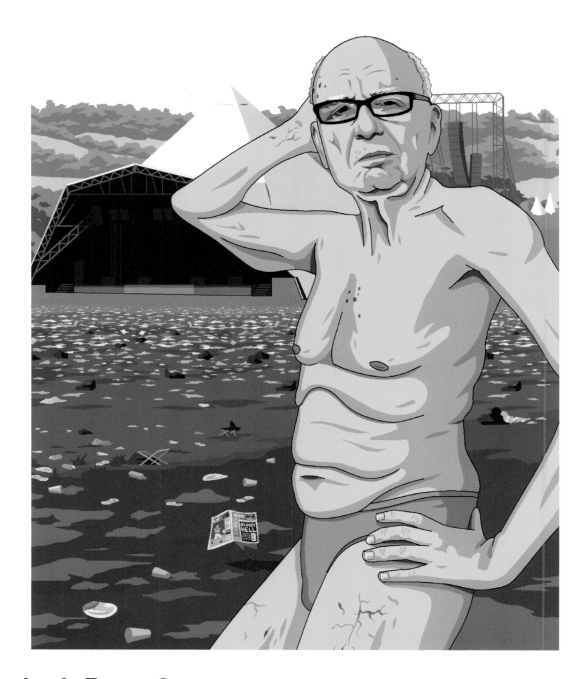

Murdoch Page 3

23 June 2016

Requested by *Glastonbury Shangri-La* newspaper

Barlow and Robo-Deirdre 4000

30 March 2017
Requested by Alex Leam

'It's the year 3998. Everybody else in the world is
dead, except for Ken Barlow and his creation Robo-
Deirdre 4000.'

Buffy the Umpire Slayer

14 March 2017
Requested by Paul Cornish

Football Coming Home

10 July 2018
Requested by Louis Simmons

'Football coming home with a bucket of vindaloo to
find his wife in bed with another sport.'

Bill Paxton Tribute

28 February 2017
Requested by Patton Oswalt (via our mutual Twitter followers)

'An Alien, a Predator and a Terminator pouring out
their forties at Bill Paxton's grave.'

Barry-O Kart

11 October 2018
Requested by Joseph Payne

'Can you paint Barry-O Kart? Basically *Mario Kart* only instead of Mario it's Barry off *EastEnders* and instead of the other Mario characters it's everyone off *EastEnders* and the whole picture has a vaguely tragic aura.'

Edd the Duck 209

29 June 2018
Requested by Robin Hill

'Edd (the Duck) 209 goes wrong in a board meeting of eighties/nineties kids' TV presenters. Andy Crane gets shot to bits, Andi Peters calls it a glitch and Phillip Schofield looks very disappointed.'

Get Well Soon, Humpty Bear

16 November 2016
Requested by Simon Barlow-Smyth

'Hi Jim! I'm currently holed up in hospital having recently undergone two major brain surgeries and I'm starting to feel like a bear in captivity! Please could you paint me as a blue-eyed anthropomorphic Baloo-esque bear, with my *Heroes*-symbol-shaped head scar visible (top, right side of head), sitting in my blue hospital chair, wearing a He-Man "I have the power" T-shirt (adorned with a large Remembrance Sunday poppy), eating a mountainous chocolate cake (à la Bruce Bogtrotter) from the white hospital trolley before me. Above my head there is a large zoo-esque painted sign which says "Humpty Bear". On the hospital bed beside me there are two large medical specimen jars; one contains an ugly tumorous growth that looks like Donald Trump and is labelled "Brian", the second jar contains a green-ish Nigel Farage-looking sludge labelled "Aero". Thank you in advance for your consideration.'

Brexit Swipe Cover

22 June 2016

Created in the week leading up to the 2016 EU referendum for short-lived internet-in-print magazine *Swipe.*

Harry Potter and the Deathly Heroin Addiction

4 March 2019

Requested by Ben Moag

'Please paint a grotty London drug scene with Harry Potter off his face on heroin with Kings Cross in the background. Instead of wands, it's needles. Sirius Black is a big black homeless dog licking Harry's face. Hagrid is a pimp wearing a shaggy fur coat and Snape is dealing drugs to Ron Weasley, who has a wasted Hermione hanging off him.'

Oddie Beats Hitler at Catchphrase

16 December 2014
Requested by Sam Stockwell

'Dear Jim,
Can you paint when Hitler was a contestant on
Catchphrase and was absolutely furious because his
opponent was Bill Oddie and all of the catchphrases
were about birds?'

Jesus Gunges God

11 December 2014
Requested by Dave Rankin

'Dave Benson Phillips helping Jesus to gunge God
on *Get Your Own Back*.'

Hollywood Berry Embrace

21 September 2016
Requested by Jay Skinner

'Paul Hollywood and Mary Berry in a tight loving embrace surrounded by an apocalyptic bake-themed kitchen with exploding sponges and flaming Battenbergs.'

Roger Moore Reunion Tribute

31 May 2017
Requested by Josman Tickle

'Roger Moore's Bond having a grand reunion party
with all the villains from the Moore era. They're all
on surprisingly good terms about the whole thing.
Blofeld is doing the catering from his delicatessen in
stainless steel.'

The One Who Knocks Twice

The image of Postman Pat in the iconic *Breaking Bad* season one poster pose is one of the better known Jim'll Paint It pieces alongside *Brian Blessed Punching a Polar Bear* and *Ross Kemp on Toast*. It was originally part of a larger image featuring Postman Pat in a variety of increasingly dark and unfortunate scenarios dreamed up by frustrated parent Joe Badham as a way of coping with his daily dose of passive Postman Pat consumption.

'Pat goes on an EDL march in Pencaster, drinks too much Skol Super and gets arrested for swearing at a police officer' was one scenario. 'Pat unwittingly makes a delivery of a large amount of heroin for the local triad gang, fucks it up as usual, mixing the package up with the one going to Mrs Goggins, who swiftly hands the drugs to the police. The triads punish Pat by cutting off his nose' was another. But it was Pat getting caught up in the events of *Breaking Bad* which endured and eventually spawned a sequel in which the roles are reversed and meth kingpin Walter White has to deliver parcels to the residents of Greendale (see page 57).

Given that four years had passed between the two pieces and my paint style had changed almost beyond recognition, I decided to quickly repaint the original Postman Pat piece so that the two complementary ideas could be displayed side by side without too jarring a discrepancy.

Postman Pat as Walter White Redux

12 May 2017
Requested by Joe Badham

With acknowledgement to John Cunliffe, creator of Postman Pat

Walter White as Postman Pat

17 May 2017
Requested by Craig Graham

'A role reversal of one of your most famous paintings with Walter White and Jesse Pinkman delivering letters and parcels and blue meth to the residents of Greendale please? With Ted Glen in the background off his tits on the meth.'

I Want to Break Free

11 April 2017
Requested by Jason Gooding

'Kryten from *Red Dwarf* recreating Queen's "I Want to Break Free" video with his groinal vacuum cleaner attachment.'

Ravers of the Lost Ark

5 December 2017
Requested by James Proctor

Ross Kemp on Toast Redux

18 February 2017
Requested by Toby Da Moose Phillips

Re-painted in celebration of four years of Jim'll Paint It.

Thatcher Rides Giant Penis

27 January 2015
Requested by Samantha Hirst

'Dear Jim,
Can you please paint Margaret Thatcher dressed
as a valkyrie, riding an enormous penis with wings
through a thunderstorm for no reason other than I
think it would be an incredibly powerful image.'

Delevingne Devo Blitz

19 March 2015
Requested by @Various_Jams

'Can you please do Cara Delevingne as every
member of Devo manning an anti-aircraft gun during
the Blitz?'

E.T. Go Home, You're Drunk

24 October 2017
Requested by Benjamin Evenden

The One Where They Enter Joey in Robot Wars

28 January 2016

Requested by Alex Pryce

Ruffling Feathers

Anyone who knows me probably also knows that I'm not the biggest fan of the British monarchy as a concept. They seem all right, on a personal level; just your average family of blundering oddballs. But I get a little bit irked by all of the ostentatious displays of extreme wealth while their subjects flounder in increasing poverty. Royal apologists always pipe up with claims that they generate tourism but France, the most visited country on earth, hasn't had a monarchy since the eighteenth century, when everyone got fed up and chopped their heads off.

Drawing a picture of the queen eating one of her swans is a far cry from demanding she be sent to the guillotine but you wouldn't think it from the reactions this picture garnered from outraged royalists. Most offended of all was a strange little man called Rob. In his staunch defence of Her Royal Highness he inexplicably started spouting hate speech about homeless people. In response, I sold this piece as a limited-edition print to raise money for Centrepoint, a charity that does amazing work supporting young homeless people.

Queen Eats Swan

21 April 2016
Requested by Jake

'Dear Jim,
Can you paint the queen savagely eating a swan?'

Dali's Surrealist Countdown

9 July 2014
Requested by Darryl

'Dear Jim,
Please paint me the final round of Salvador Dali's surrealist version of *Countdown*. One of the contestants is Danny Dyer and the other is the ghost of some Swiss cheese. Naturally the clock has melted and Danny's head has exploded whilst attempting to solve a particularly surreal crucial conundrum.'

Minions Dystopia

14 July 2015

Requested by Kevin Weaver

'Dear Jim,
Can you use Paint to show us a scene from a not-too-distant future in which those fucking Minion things have finally taken over completely?'

With acknowledgement to Pierre Coffin and Chris Renaud, creators of the Minions

Alien Queen Dropbox Bollocking

21 May 2015
Requested by @FabulousGadalf

'Dear Jim,
Please paint me the Alien Queen, back off maternity
leave and bollocking everyone for not using Dropbox
properly.'

Jong-un Surfs Trump's Hair

21 November 2017
Requested by Robin Hayles

'Kim Jong-un in stained Y-fronts, holding candyfloss
whilst surfing on a giant golden wave which is
actually Trump's hair.'

Gruber Earns His God Damn 20 Per Cent

19 January 2016
Requested by Andrew Johnson

'Dear Jim,
I'm sure you've had thousands of these, but if you
could do one of Alan Rickman, as Hans Gruber,
sitting on a beach earning his god damn 20 per cent,
that'd be grand.'

Santa Bono

4 December 2014
Requested by James Smith

'Bono dressed as Santa shoving U2 CDs down chimneys.'

Nic Cage Mount Rushmore

20 June 2017
Requested by Nick Butler

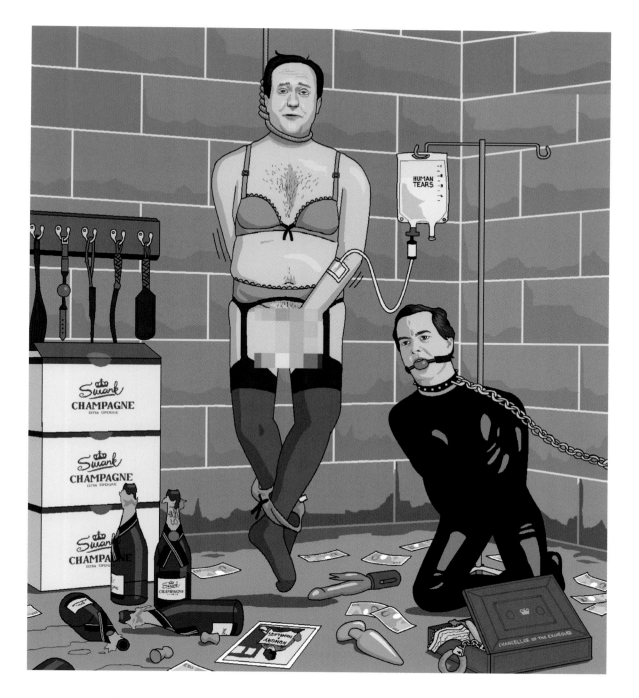

Cameron Strangle Wank

11 May 2015
Requested by Robert Robert

'David Cameron having a good old-fashioned
strangle wank to celebrate his election victory.'

Nineties Child

This was, at the time, the most ambitious piece I had ever attempted. I was given a week to complete it by an agency working for *National Geographic* to help publicise an upcoming documentary on the nineties. The brief was simply a long list of nineties cultural icons and I had absolutely no idea how to approach it. I just began drawing the top half of each figure with a view to pasting them into a new document and stitching them together in a suitably nineties scene (a warehouse rave). While MS Paint does, sort of, allow you to resize, doing so creates messy, glitchy-looking pixel issues which I thought best to avoid. As such

the finished piece has a distinctly 'Where's Wally'-esque lack of perspective.

I particularly enjoyed populating the foreground with staples from my own nineties childhood such as my beloved *GoldenEye 64* cartridge, my first ever mobile phone – a blue Nokia 3110 – and, of course, Pogs. I was fortunate enough to realise a childhood dream last year and release my own set of Pogs called Jimmos. They came in a sealed foil bag with a checklist card and holographic 'shinies'. Contrary to every expectation I had, all 200 sets sold in less than twenty-four hours.

90s Warehouse Rave

7 August 2014
Requested by National Geographic Channel

Mad Max Cola Wars

19 December 2017
Requested by Jamie Baynham

'Dear Jim,
For Christmas could I have Mad Max protecting the
Coca-Cola truck from an assault by competing soft
drink providers (Pepsi, Cresta, Barr, Panda Pops, etc.)?
He has to escort it to Chesterfield for some reason.'

Away in a Pret a Manger

11 December 2018
Requested by fatpete_86 (via Twitter)

Thomas the Flesh Abomination

24 February 2017
Requested by Adam Hughes

'Could you please paint Thomas the Tank Engine, made of flesh (except for his wheels) with a face that reflects the agony of being twisted into the shape of a train. While the Fat Controller laughs beside a pile of failed flesh locomotive experiments?'

Bert and Ernie Fear and Loathing

18 August 2015
Requested by Sam Richards

'Please could you paint Bert and Ernie taking a trip
to Vegas – à la *Fear and Loathing* – with Elmo as
their petrified hitchhiker?'

With acknowledgement to Jim and Jane Henson, creators of the Muppets

Pennywise IT Guy

31 October 2017
Requested by Chris Gosdin

'Pennywise the clown working as the department
IT guy and being overburdened with tech support
work.'

Partridge Thriller

18 November 2014
Requested by Paul

'Dear Jim,
I would like to know what Michael Jackson's
"Thriller" video would have looked like had all the
zombies been Alan Partridge.'

Awkward Star Trek Orgy

24 July 2014
Requested by Sam Wise

Washed-Up Sonic

27 April 2017

Requested by David Sinclair

'A bitter, washed-up Sonic the Hedgehog on crutches drowning his sorrows in a bar having completely ruined his knees with twenty-six years of high-impact running. He's crying over a tattered photo of Amy Rose and has just spent his last gold ring on whiskey.'

With acknowledgement to Hirokazu Yasuhara, creator of Sonic the Hedgehog

Slasher Shopping

29 October 2015
Requested by Faye Andrews

'Freddy, Jason, Michael Myers and Ghostface in Tesco ransacking the Halloween display and trying on masks of each other. They're all making fun of Candyman because there aren't any costumes of him and he's in the background being comforted by the Tesco greeter and some old dears.'

May Trump Dirty Dancing

18 July 2018
Requested by Jason O Hanlon

'Dear Jim,
Can you paint me Theresa May and Donald Trump re-enacting that famous scene from *Dirty Dancing* in the lake... you know the one I'm on about. Maybe throw in a few circling sharks for the craic and Trump wearing some inflatable armbands to keep him afloat.'

Chestburster Puppets

13 September 2016
Requested by ealadubhsidhe

'Dear Jim,
Could you please paint the "chestburster" scene
from *Alien* as portrayed by famous TV puppets, with
Zippy from *Rainbow* as John Hurt being held down
as a human hand bursts through his stomach.'

Paul Daniels' Stag Party

5 February 2015
Requested by Glenn

'Dear Jim,
Can you paint me Paul Daniels on his stag night in his home town Middlesbrough? He is dressed as Wonder Woman and handcuffed to a dwarf in a tuxedo who is slightly taller than him. The only other person on the stag is Louis Theroux in a Bananaman costume. They are standing in the rain having just been ejected from a nightclub and Paul looks both geographically and spiritually lost.'

Bizarrely, this image was banned from Facebook, presumably because of Louis Theroux's blow-up sex doll. Strange to think that we still live in a world where the female nipple is so shocking and offensive that even a cartoon image of a doll's breast is deemed too risqué for public consumption. By contrast, Facebook had no such issue with my portrayal of men (with their nipples on show) falling from the sky and bursting into puddles of bone and gore.

Thom Yorke the Tank Engine

1 April 2016
Requested by Joe Ereaut

It's Literally Raining Men

12 April 2018
Requested by Anthony Mitchell

'The Weather Girls gleefully performing their most famous hit, "It's Raining Men", whilst surrounded by a scene of absolute carnage as the bodies of the unfortunate aforementioned men lie dead and dying around them, having inexplicably fallen from the sky. Meanwhile, Michael Fish and Siân Lloyd look on, bewildered.'

A Brush with Death

On 24 July 2017 Windows announced that it would be axing Paint in its latest system update. Touchingly, as if a close family member had died, scores of people sent me their heartfelt condolences via social media. There were also many requests involving Paint ascending into Windows heaven to join all of the other obsolete software. The news was never going to impact my work as I'd been running the older XP version of Paint (my favourite version of the software) on a virtual machine ever since my actual XP desktop packed in. But it was truly sad to see the official end of such an iconic program. Given how pivotal Paint had been in both my career and personal life I immediately began working on a tribute.

The very next day, just as I was putting the finishing touches on the piece, it was announced that, following a huge backlash from the program's many fans, Paint wasn't being axed after all and would instead be available for free via the Windows Store. Rather than bin the work I'd already done I tweaked the text in Clippy's speech bubble to make it an illustration about a near-death experience. In many ways, it's the best of both worlds. Paint lives on and I got to spend a day in my happy place, drawing all the forgotten characters from Windows' colourful past.

Windows Heaven

25 July 2017
Requested by Martin Kidd

Stalked by Wogan

3 June 2015
Requested by Chris

'Dear Jim,
My mate Andy is convinced he is being stalked by
Terry Wogan. Can you please paint what it's like to
be stalked by Terry Wogan?'

Alien Loves Predator

3 July 2014
Requested by Matthew Hawkins

'Predator and Alien skipping down the beach hand
in hand.'

The Great British Grind Off

14 October 2016

Dreadful

9 January 2019
Requested by Raised by Owls

Cover artwork for comedy grindcore band Raised By Owls' debut album and their subsequent follow up. Both pieces take inspiration from the titles of songs such as 'The Phillip Schofield Chainsaw Massacre', 'You've Been Mary Buried' and 'Cliff Richard Drinks from the Skulls of His Enemies'.

Smeagol Discovers H. Samuel

7 October 2014
Requested by Leilah Skelton

Books Are My Bag, a nationwide campaign to celebrate and support bookshops, enlisted my help to raise awareness for the cause by running a competition where people could submit literary-based suggestions for me to paint. This was the winning suggestion.

Doctor Who Marries a Dalek

13 July 2017
Requested by Jim Murray

Quaid and Damon Enjoy Mars Water

6 October 2015
Requested by Brian Pope

'Dear Jim,
To celebrate NASA's findings of water on Mars could you please paint Douglas Quaid off of *Total Recall* (1990 obviously) and Matt Damon off of the new film *The Martian* enjoying a lovely refreshing glass of mineral water in a Martian desert sat on a couple of lovely old wingback chesterfields. Quaid is wearing his rotund lady suit and has had to open the face so he can drink. Damon can be wearing anything you want.'

Paint It Black

10 June 2016
Requested by Jack Davis

'Dear Jim,
Could you please paint Mick Jagger disappointing
customers at the paint mixing station in B&Q by
matching every colour as black?'

Werner the Herzog

25 November 2017
Requested by James Field

Clever Girl

3 November 2016
Requested by Mark

'Dear Jim,
Could you please paint a picture of the velociraptor
from *Jurassic Park* being a "clever girl" and absolutely
smashing her exams with Richard Attenborough and
Jeff Goldblum looking very proud.'

Wolverine Stuck in a Catflap

23 June 2014
Requested by Jeff Stubbs

Rooney Can't Potato

27 February 2015
Requested by Nick Travis

'Wayne Rooney trying to peel a potato.'

Painted into a Corner

This is one of those pictures I painted just for the sheer therapy of it. At the time I was feeling a little overwrought. Until relatively recently I'd put myself under a needless amount of stress, deluding myself that my financial security was exclusively sustained and my existence validated by my turning out at least one new picture every week. Half of my time was spent joylessly scrolling through requests desperately trying to find one funny or original enough to paint, feeling as if the whole world would implode if I didn't pick the right one and get it painted immediately. I've chilled out a bit since then but it's funny to think how catastrophising and other cognitive distortions can turn a dream job into a nightmare.

That said, whenever I actually pick something and start painting I remember why I enjoy doing this so much and all the stress melts away. This is especially true when creating oozing Cronenberg-esque monsters. The Trump monster is playing *Pokémon GO*, which was the craze of the time, and the inclusion of Bear Grylls grilling a bear was a nod to my close friends who'd tease me with it after I once grumbled that someone sends me that request (or some permutation of it) virtually every week. It's easy to become jaded and lose sight of just how lucky I am to receive hundreds of ideas every week, even if some of them are the same.

I'm wearing exactly what I was wearing the day I started painting it. I bought those burger-print Vans after I saw my godson, Otis, wearing the same pair and was delighted to discover they did them in grown-up sizes. Perhaps people who don't get their style tips from two-year-olds cope better with the stresses of adult life and don't have to resort to concocting grotesque Chuckle Brother monsters as therapy.

Tormented Self-Portrait

19 July 2016
Requested by Paddy Harley

'Dear Jim,
How about you paint yourself into a corner? Literally: a representation of you cowering in fear in the corner of a dark room, paint covering every surface except the patch where you are, with twisted monsters, politicians and nineties TV stars bearing down on you from every direction. A grim summation of the internet artist's burden as he realises he can't please everybody.'

ThunderCats and Thunderbirds

25 November 2018
Requested by Adam Barnsley

'Dear Jim,
Can you please paint a picture of the ThunderCats
terrorising the Thunderbirds? One of the Tracys
could be up a tree; Lion-O could be presenting a
mauled Brains as a present, like a good kitty.'

With acknowledgement to Tobin Wolf, creator of *ThunderCats*; and Gerry and Sylvia Anderson, creators of *Thunderbirds*

Kenan and Kellraiser

7 May 2018
Requested by Matt Sweetmore

Zero G Fawlty Towers

8 April 2015
Requested by Dave Sanders

'Dear Jim,
Please paint an episode of *Fawlty Towers* in zero gravity.'

Lovely Christmas Dinner

15 December 2016
Requested by Benjamin Allen

'Please paint Kevin McCallister, George Bailey, Bob Cratchit (Kermit version), Buddy the Elf and the Snowman having a lovely Christmas dinner together while a shivering John McClane solemnly watches from outside the dining-room window.'

Foxes Hunt May

8 June 2017
Requested by Andy Welch

'Please can you paint Fox McCloud from *Star Fox* in his Arwing fighter, Miles "Tails" Prower in his biplane, and the cyborg ninja Gray Fox from *Metal Gear Solid* chasing down Theresa May whilst Brian May and some badgers cheer them on?'

Barry Scott Overenthusiastic Undertaker

2 August 2016

Requested by Barrie Mason

'Barry Scott of Cillit Bang fame as an overenthusiastic undertaker trying to sell coffins to a bereaved family. Purple coffins, before and after corpses and the obligatory "BANG" as he slams a lid down.'

Cameron Miss Piggy

22 September 2015
Requested by Duncan Jay

'Kermit the Frog defending Miss Piggy from David
Cameron.'

With acknowledgement to Jim and Jane Henson, creators of the Muppets

Michael Owen Forced Cool Runnings

17 October 2017
Requested by Chris Stitt

'Michael Owen once tweeted that he's only ever
seen eight films and that he was "forced" to watch,
among others, *Cool Runnings*. Please paint Michael
Owen being literally forced to watch *Cool Runnings*.'

David Blaine Cavity Search

15 March 2019

Requested by Paddy O'Donnell

'Dear Jim,
Can you do a painting of David Blaine being cavity
checked by airport security only for them to find a
long chain of brightly coloured handkerchiefs in his
rectum?'

Nightmare Trump Grabs Pussies

25 October 2016
Requested by Stephen Buxton

'How about Trump trying to grab some terrified pussy cats down a dark alley. Maybe with those freaky long arms Freddy has in *Nightmare on Elm Street*?'

Donkey Birthday Party

12 January 2017
Requested by Leo Nicoletti

'How about a children's birthday party set in an alternate universe where donkeys evolved to be the dominant species? There's a few children playing a version of Buckaroo involving a plastic human man where you have to load him up with little plastic thought bubbles that contain words/phrases such as "inferiority complex", "social anxiety" and "money issues". In the background we can see children playing "pin the tail on the man" (obviously the "tail" will have to be blurred). Finally, there are a few blindfolded children with baseball bats trying to smack the sweets out of a papier-mâché representation of a Mexican man.'

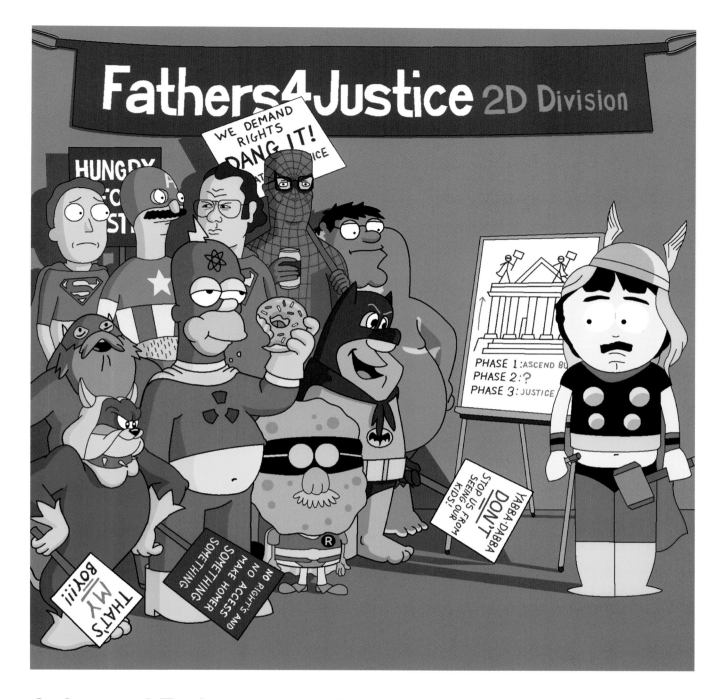

Animated Fathers 4 Justice

18 January 2017
Requested by William Large

'Dear Jim,
Could you paint various animated dads, such as Fred Flintstone and Homer Simpson, planning a Fathers 4 Justice rally? Their superhero costumes are all the wrong sizes.'

With acknowledgement to Loren Bouchard, creator of *Bob's Burgers*; Matt Groening, creator of *The Simpsons*; William Hanna and Joseph Barbera, creators of *The Flintstones* and *Tom and Jerry*; Mike Judge and Greg Daniels, creators of *King of the Hill*; Seth MacFarlane, creator of *Family Guy*; Trey Parker and Matt Stone, creators of *South Park*

Simon Adelman

During Christmas 2016 my wife started volunteering with the Marmalade Trust, a local Bristol-based charity focussed on bringing companionship to elderly and vulnerable people who would otherwise be alone on Christmas Day. During the drive to raise money for their Christmas lunch social I offered to help out by auctioning off the chance to have me paint a picture of anything the highest bidder desired.

The winner of the auction, Peter Sherwood, came back to me after Christmas with a beautifully simple idea about celebrity chefs (seriously, what is it about celebrity chefs?) desperately trying to get his young son Jack to eat his dinner. He also wanted his friend Simon Adelman to feature somewhere wearing an 'I'm Simon Adelman' T-shirt.

Simon Adelman was an instant hit with Jim'll Paint It followers and has since become something of a 'Where's Wally' character, popping up in the background of many paints since. His iconic sky-blue T-shirt was even available to buy from the Jim'll Paint It shop, resulting in real life 'Simon Adelman' spottings in Massachusetts, the Giant's Causeway and even hanging out with Donatella Versace.

For more information about the Marmalade Trust visit marmaladetrust.org.

Frustrated Chefs

4 January 2017
Requested by Peter Sherwood

'Could you please paint the time when Heston Blumenthal, Gordon Ramsay and Jamie Oliver couldn't get my son Jack to eat his dinner? The chefs got frustrated and started to turn on each other. Jamie Oliver was crying (again).

If possible, do you think you could please include a cameo of my friend Simon Adelman?'

Fight for Whiteley

24 March 2016
Requested by Dave Sanderson

'Carol Vorderman and Rachel Riley having a fight
over a sexy Richard Whiteley.'

Craig Charles Refbot Awkward Date

17 December 2015
Requested by Chris Redgate

'Dear Jim,
Please paint Craig Charles and Refbot having an
awkward time on Channel 4's *First Dates*.'

Trump Piers Greggs Date

14 February 2018
Requested by Amy Bee Sting

'Dear Jim,
Please, please paint me Donald Trump and Piers
Morgan having a date in Greggs on Valentine's Day.'

Dodgy Alan Sugar

2 March 2018

Requested by Ben Dc

'Alan Sugar selling broken old Amstrads and knock-off Spurs gear from a yellow three-wheeler.'

Reservoir Dogs Retro Toys

30 June 2014
Requested by Matt

'Dear Jim,
I would like to see *Reservoir Dogs* recreated with
the cast riding space-hoppers, pogo sticks, roller
blades, Bernie Clifton-style ostriches and anything
else that takes your fancy.'

Bowie Tribute
11 January 2016

Celeb Blender

Jim's Celeb Blender was an experimental image generator created by Ian Ravenscroft and Joseph Bell for BBC Taster. The idea was that users could select from a list of locations, celebrities and bizarre activities to create their own instant Jim'll Paint It-style tableau complete with accompanying dramatic narration by John Henry Falle.

Of course, this involved spending many weeks painting my way through a huge list of assets. As well as various background locations, each celebrity had to be depicted doing a variety of outlandish activities

such as shooting fire from a saxophone or weightlifting a dolphin. My early paints had been characterised by a kind of goofy randomness where celebrities and situations seemed almost entirely arbitrary and interchangeable. The Celeb Blender allowed me to take this side of my work to its logical conclusion and, while I'm hugely proud of how it turned out, I've since erred towards subjects that have an internal logic of their own.

It was launched in April 2016 and ran until October 2018.

Clarkson Can't McDonald's

31 March 2015
Requested by Robert Betts

'Jeremy Clarkson getting fired from his new job as a McDonald's trainee.'

Abu Hamza

22 July 2014
Requested by Ben Amodio

'Abu Hamza trying to change a duvet cover.'

Brunel Awkward Threesome Refusal

29 November 2016
Requested by Jamie Gwalcherfen Green

'Dear Jim,
Please could you paint Isambard Kingdom Brunel awkwardly refusing a threesome from an elderly couple in a caravan, whilst a completely unprepared chicken, feathers and all, cooks in the oven.'

Kebabba the Hutt

20 April 2017
Requested by Andrew Sanders

'Dear Jim,
Please paint an intergalactic chip shop. A high street outlet on a Friday night/Saturday morning, with various characters from *Star Wars* queued for chips and kebabs, served by Jabba the Hutt, whilst Chewbacca is being sick outside, R2-D2 is on his back drunk and Han Solo and Boba Fett are arguing over a taxi in the shape of an X-wing. In the night sky the Death Star looms ready to vaporise the entire planet. Thank you very much.'

Painting Frank

This piece was painted as a tribute to Frank Kelly, who had sadly passed away that week. Despite the sombre circumstances, it was one of my all-time favourites to paint. It's always a huge bonus when I know and love the source material I'm parodying and can add in lots of additional references such as the pet brick, the lovely girls, the missing Lourdes money and the Golden Cleric award. It proved to be one of the most popular pieces I've ever painted, thanks entirely to *Father Ted*'s status as a beloved hallmark of comedy and especially Kelly's portrayal of Father Jack.

I was, at the time, deeply humbled that the piece had won the approval of the show's co-creator Graham Linehan. This was long before he, upsettingly, began devoting his life to being angry about transgender people on Twitter and lost the respect that I, and many others, once had for him.

Father Jack Arrives

2 March 2016
Requested by James Sheppard

'Dear Jim,
I would love to see Father Ted's peaceful eighteen
years in heaven being disturbed by the arrival of
Father Jack being chased by glasses-stealing
crows.'

Boba Fett Competition

29 April 2016
Requested by Manny McArthur

'Danny DeVito losing a Boba Fett costume competition to some children.'

Kittens and Favourite Things

26 April 2018

Requested by A Guy Hamilton

'Kittens. Just a big group of kittens goofing around, mate.

They can be playing in and around all sorts of culture references, band T-shirts, discarded placards, whatever you want. In fact – better than that – pick all your favourite things and put them in there;

favourite chocolate bar, favourite album, favourite T-shirt, a toy from your childhood…

But kittens. Playing. A fair few of them mucking about.

That's all.'

House Robots vs Chelsea

3 February 2017
Requested by Tom Hackwell

'Dear Jim,
Please could you paint the carnage that ensued when the commentator Jonathan Pearce merged realities and commentated on a Premier League football match between the cast of house robots from *Robot Wars* and Chelsea?'

Modzilla vs Gothra

12 February 2016
Requested by Daniel Simpson Day

Darth May

15 July 2016
Requested by Sam Trenery

'Theresa May as Darth Vader with Thatcher as the
emperor, giving her orders via hologram.'

Coronation Street Fighter II Redux

7 November 2017
Requested by Rhys Herdman

Mary Berry's Frankenstein

20 September 2017
Requested by Clare Logan

Schofield Willoughby Psychotic Episode

11 December 2018

Requested by fatpete_86 (via Twitter)

'Please paint Phillip Schofield and Holly Willoughby having hysterically laughed themselves so hard they've slipped into a psychotic episode and destroyed the set of *This Morning*, and murdered the crew and any guests (including Katie Hopkins?).

Gino D'Acampo is trying to use a baking tray as a shield and a spatula as a weapon to fend off Holly, who's about to bludgeon him to death with a handful of uncooked spaghetti.'

Mr Bump Pile-up
28 October 2014
Requested by Matty

'Mr Bump giving a statement to a police officer
following a multi-car pile-up on the M4.'

With acknowledgement to Roger Hargreaves, creator of Mr Bump

The Wu-Tang Clangers

29 May 2018
Requested by Roland Whiteley

Trump Carves Rushmore

14 January 2016
Requested by Beth Wingrove

'Donald Trump furtively carving his own face into the
side of Mount Rushmore while being attacked by a
pair of eagles.'

Dibnah Demolishes Barad-dûr

15 November 2016
Requested by smit1977z (via Instagram)

'Fred Dibnah knocking down Sauron's Tower.'

Happiness

After a run of particularly dark and bleak paints my friend Sam Wise suggested I paint an interpretation of pure happiness. So, of course, I drew a picture of two cockatiels playing *GoldenEye 64*.

Cockatiels are my absolute favourite creatures in the world. They're so pure and full of character. I would happily watch YouTube videos of them for hours on end. I even have a tattoo of one on my arm.

I'm also a big fan of old video games and, for me, the Nintendo 64 represents the apex of a beautiful but short-lived era where ambition and creativity was at an all-time high, often far exceeding the technical limitations of the hardware. Small teams of developers would approach game design with the playful naivety of a child handed a strange and unfamiliar toy. The resulting games had enough explorative potential and graphical realism to be completely engaging while the unavoidable polygons and fog lent everything an abstract, dreamlike quality.

Of course, I'm just an ageing man, waxing nostalgic about his favourite childhood game. But it really is quite hard to imagine in today's age of online gaming and cynical micro transactions that anyone could experience the simple, socially bonding joy of sitting beside your best friend as you blast their polygonal counterpart in the face with a fully loaded RC-P90. Someone pass me my slippers.

GoldenEye Cockatiels

3 August 2016
Requested by Sam Wise

'Dear Jim,
Please paint pure happiness.'

Stephen Hawking Star Trek Tribute

21 March 2018
Requested by Ray Hamill

'Dear Jim,
Please can you paint a classic *Star Trek* starship bridge with Stephen Hawking sitting in the captain's chair whilst the other positions are occupied by Marie Curie, Albert Einstein, George Washington Carver, Galileo Galilei and Dorothy Hodgkin. They have been reunited in the afterlife to continue improving science for the benefit of all humanity by boldly going where no late genius has gone before.'

Attenborough vs Cthulhu

14 November 2017
Requested by Jim Taylor

'Dear Jim,
Can you please paint Sir David Attenborough
battling the dark lord Cthulhu during the filming of an
episode of *Blue Planet* for the BBC?'

Botham Defends Against Stormtroopers

24 September 2015
Requested by Craig Andrew Lynn

'Dear Jim,
Can you please paint Ian Botham defending himself
from stormtrooper laser blasts with a cricket bat?'

Art Attack

12 May 2016
Requested by Simon Ovenden

'The day Neil Buchanan lost his mind and attempted to make a Big Art Attack of his own face from human viscera and body parts.'

Theatre of Dreams

6 February 2019
Requested by Adrian Steel

'My wife and I got married on the centre spot at Wembley Stadium. I'm also obsessed with Kylie Minogue and 70s cop drama *The Sweeney* (so much so that my sons' names are Carter and Regan). Can you please therefore paint a scene at Wembley where I'm putting in a perfect cross to my wife, who's just out-jumped Carter and Regan to put a smashing header past goalkeeper Kylie Minogue. David Beckham and Stuart Pearce have already started to celebrate.'

With acknowledgement to William Hanna and Joseph Barbera, creators of *Wacky Races*; and Shigeru Miyamoto, creator of *Super Mario Kart*

Snarface

8 January 2019

Requested by Matt Gibbs

'Like what the fuck is a Snarf? … Fuck him' *Jim'll Paint It, November 2018*

'I am Snarf. Protector of the crap sidekick, defender of the oppressed. I am Snarface. Dick Dastardly has had enough of Muttley's shit and is beating him mercilessly. Various other crap sidekicks such as Godzooky and Scrappy-Doo are next in line for a beating.

Snarface (yes, me in a poorly fitting Snarf costume and face caked with charlie) has come to the rescue in full-on "Stay away from my little friend!" mode, while my family look on in confusion.

Godzilla is in a rage having misplaced Godzooky, and is attacking the Clifton Suspension Bridge in the background.'

Optimus Amazon Prime

21 August 2018
Requested by Josie Hypatia Grounds

Dickinson's Real Drug Deal

2 June 2016
Requested by Ryan Corder

Bono Geldof Christmas Tax Evasion

12 December 2017
Requested by Chris Adamson

'Please can you make a picture of Bono arriving in Africa to let them know it's Christmas time, only to be greeted by the Inland Revenue [sic] holding unpaid tax invoices. With Bob Geldof having already arrived, crying in the background because they have repossessed his Feed the World T-shirt?'

Tory Squat Party
28 March 2018
Requested by Matt Durstan Tilke

'Tory squat party. Boris has a nosebleed from snorting too much speed, May is drinking Special Brew and Hunt is burning the Criminal Justice Bill while Farage, in full hunting gear, is calling the police.'

Mike Myers Confusion

2 August 2018
Requested by Dave Rankin

'There's been some confusion and various Mike
Myers characters are stalking the residents of
Haddonfield.'

Kanye Birth
25 September 2018
Requested by Maria Panda Williamson

'Can you paint Kanye West giving birth to Kanye
West whilst Kim Kardashian feeds him Walkers
cheese and onion crisps on a bed of brie?'

Trump Sashay Away

26 January 2017
Requested by Adam Godding

'Dear Jim,
Please can you paint Trump, Pence, William Pryor and other anti-LGBT folk in Trump's senatorial candidate list dressed in drag on a RuPaul-esque drag show with Obama as RuPaul telling them to sashay away!'

Prince Philip Driving
25 January 2018
Requested by Peter Jeffrey

'How about Theresa May throwing Jeremy Corbyn's severed head in the air while she, Boris Johnson and Jacob Rees-Mogg stand up through the sunroof in a Union Jack-painted limousine being driven off the White Cliffs of Dover by Prince Philip?'

Eighties Baby

Given how much I'd enjoyed creating the nineties pop culture paint for *National Geographic*, it had been at the back of my mind to give the eighties – the decade that spawned both MS Paint and myself – a similar treatment. A celebration of the myriad cultural hallmarks, from *Ghostbusters* to Madonna, that it's now hard to imagine a world without.

I was an eighties baby, nineties child, so my perception of the decade is probably very different from those who actually lived through the bleakest days of Thatcherism and Reaganism. For my generation, the eighties is an abstraction patched together from videotapes and hand-me-down toys, creating a nostalgia for an era that never really happened. This faux-nostalgia manifests itself in 'synthwave' music, films such as *Drive* and *Kung Fury* and video games like *Blood Dragon* and

Hotline Miami. I'm a huge fan of that hyper-eighties neon and chrome aesthetic so I was keen to try and capture that spirit and channel it into this paint, giving me a rare chance to use a more stylised colour palette full of rich oranges, pinks and purples.

It took three solid weeks of work to finish and contains at least eighty cultural references. When I began work on it, I'd just returned from a trip to New York and thought Times Square would make an ideal background and give me plenty of opportunities to fit additional eighties icons on the giant neon advertisements. The hardest part was probably resisting the urge to keep squeezing in more things.

In the space of three months it outsold every other paint I've done.

80s
13 September 2018

Dafoe

26 May 2016
Requested by 71394 (via Tumblr)

'Willem Dafoe wearing a bright purple helmet riding
a little girl's bike away from a burning city.'

Acknowledgements

This book, and every painting inside it, owes its existence to my best friend, travel companion and loving wife, Natalie. For fifteen years she has encouraged all of my artistic endeavours, held my hand through the darkest days and laughed with me through the best. I couldn't have done any of this without her.

I also owe a great debt to all of my family and friends for their love, support and wisdom, especially my mum for being my number one fan from the very start, my dad for always keeping my best interests at heart, Alan and Wendy for the bacon sandwiches and Cooper for keeping me company during the day.

Thank you to Richard Flanagan, Tim Silver, Jim Witts, Ellis Covington and everyone else at Tshirtify for their hard work and support in forging this hobby into a living. Thanks, for much the same reasons, to Dominic Greyer, James Woodley, Ben Ellefsen, Joseph Bell and Ian Ravenscroft.

Finally, thanks to Beth Lewis, Imogen Denny, everyone at Unbound and all the people who believed in this book and pledged their hard-earned cash to make it a reality.

Helen Hammond
Lee Hampton
Matthew Hancock
Trish Hann
Tony Hanna
Tom Hannan
Alison Hanratty
Peter Hanson
Donna Hardcastle
Richard Harding
John Hards
Chris Hargreaves
Keith Harland
Antonia Harman
Andrew Harris
Cyriak Harris
Geoff Harris
Harry Harris
Helen Harris
Jess Harris
Rhodri Harris
Robin Harrison
Tim Harrow
Helen Harvey
Mark Harviston
Jessica Hastings
Chris Hatton
Andreas Hauger
Luke Hawkins
Peter Hawkins
Joey Hayes
Matt Hayhurst
Thomasin Hazelden
Thom Heald
Matthew Heap
Lauren Heath
Ryan Heath
Lloyd Hegarty
Ian Hegerty
Gavin Heggs
Thomas (unbound)
    Henderson
Nick Henson
Michael Heritage
Adam Hewett
Steven Hewitson
Colin Heyworth
Catherine Hickey
Steve Hicks
Martin Higginson
Anthony Highton
Brian Hildebrand
Carly Hill
Phil Hill
Simon Himsworth
Daniel Hinchcliffe
Adam Hinchliffe
Laura Hine
Jay Hirst
Joanna Hockenhull

Mike Hockey
Ben Hodder
Calum Hodgetts
Luke Hodgson
Martin Hodgson
Louise Hollands
Lawrence Holloway
Emma Holohan
Mark Honeyborne
Jack Hooley
Damien Hopkins
Richard Hopkins
Emma Hopkinson
Levi ten out of ten Horth
Ben Howard
Peter Howarth
Alex Howe
Steven Howe
Tony Howells
James Bubba Howle
Jason Howle
Tony Howse
Darren Hubbard
Rob Huckle
Liam Hudson
Michael Hudson
Alex Hughes
Katie Hughes
Robyn Hughes
Tom Hughes
Paul Hulme
Oliver & Laura Humpage
Alex Humphreys
Adam Huninik
Adam Hunt
Alan Hunt
Parker Hunt
Matt Hunter
Marc Hurds
Mike Hurst
Fabian Huss
Nyssa Hutchings
Lindsay Hutchinson
Tom Hutchinson
Ian's Little Bro
Maria Idle
Ben Iredale
Andrew Irvine
Laurence Irvine
Roan Irving
Jonathan Ives
Craig Jacobs
Vaaris Jadeja
David James
James James
Luke James
Mike James
Stuart James
Peter Jarvis
Tim Jarvis

Malcolm Jeff
Laura Jellicoe
Peter Jennings
Tom Jessiman
Phil Jewell
Andy Johns
Dale Johnson
Pete Johnson
Ste Johnson
Wayne Johnson
Emmy Maddy Johnston
Tom Jonas-Mawji
Dave H Jones
Dean Jones
Jason Jones
John Jones
Kelly Jones
Peter Jones
Rhiannon Jones
Simon Jones
Steve Jones
Westleigh Jones
Alex Jordan
Hiren Joshi
Nikki Joyce
Zeibura Kathau
Rob Kay
Tom Keating
Aiden Shane Keenan
Sean Kelly
Sian Kelly
Adam Kemeny
Ben Kemp
Paul Kemp
Nicola & Jeremy Kennon
Rhys Kent
Andrew Kettlewell
Dan Kieran
Daniel Kilburn
Matt Kille
Michael Killeen
Brenton Kilroy
Darren King
David King
James King
Jon King
Matt King
Arthur King Bowie
Pete Kitchen
Stephen Kitchin
Nick Kitchin & Lauren Grest
Chad Knight
James Knight
Philip Knight
Peter Knowles
Raymond Ko
Georgy Kolosov
    Stimcent v.d.
Krachthoefener
Jan Kuhlmann

Ben Labowstin
John Lacey
Duncan Ladkin
Anthony Lagomarsino
Jennifer Lamb
Carl Lane
Peter Lant
Steven Larry
Bill Latham
Jon Laurie
David Lawrence
Jimmy Leach
Mark Leach
Darren Lean
Duncan Leatherdale
Reubenn Leatherland
Marc Lebailly
Andy Lee
Paul Lee
Wayne Leech
Sam Leftley
Michael Leftwich
Andy Leppard
Charlie Big Spuds -
    LeVerrier
Ben Lewis
Matt Lewis
Paul Lewis
Chris Leworthy
Kerry Li / David AllardNecati
Liam loves Elspeth
Louise Lightfoot
Jonathan Lines
Nick Lines
James Little
Jamie Livingstone
Barry Lloyd
James Lockwood
Nick Lockwood
Alec Logie
Richard Logue
Lolbert K. Lolzworth
    @Lolbertz
Aj Lornie
Joe Lount
Michael Lowe
Simon Lucas
Aled Lumley Jones
Dan Lyness
Éanna MacAonghusa
Iain MacCalman
Violet Macdonald
Craig MacGregor
Siobhan Mackenzie
Gayle Maclean
Calum MacLeod
Alex MacPhee
Robert MacRory-Crowley
Simon Maddy
Arlie Magenis

Adam Mager
Claudine Mahu
James Mahy
James Malcolm
Ben Malhi
Sean Malone
Amy Maloy
Christopher "Chris" Man
Barry Mangham
Ed Manning
George Marchand
Alan Markey
Ben Marlow
Jennifer Marr
Michael 'Moose' Marriott
Chris Marsh
Phillip Marsh
Chris Marshall
Oliver Marshall
Zeke Marshall
Graham Martin
Israel Martin
Stuart Masheder
Barry Mason
Pip Mason
Ben Masters
Nikhil Masters
From Matthew
Liam Matthews
Simon Matthews
Josh Maunder
George Mayes-Milner
Chris Mayfield
Gary McBeth
Chris McBride
Andrew McColvin
James McConnell
Joey McConnell-Farber
Mike McCormack
Wayne McCrystal
Michael McCue
Paddy McCusker
Duncan McDade
Brian McDermott
Chris McDermott
Martin McDermott
Drew & Cara McDougall
Kirstin McDougall
Ricky McDowall
Fiona McDowell
Sophie McEwan
Paddy McFadden
Jordan McFall
Andrew McFeeters
John McGarrigle
Steve McGarry
Stuart McGillivray
Chris McGinness
Ben McGowan
Ciara McGrattan

Michael McGuire
David McHugh
Alexander McIntosh
Christian McKay
Jennifer McLaughlin
Mark McLaughlin
David McLean
Helen McLean
Susan McLoughlin
Gary McMurray
Jim McNally
Lucy McNeil
Adam Mead
Colin Meechan
Nick Mellish
Andy Menham
Ben Merrick
Alun Metcalf
Dan Metcalfe
Jamie Metherell
Kris Middleton
Ben Midson
Milan Milanov
Darren Paul Miller
Graham Miller
Ken Miller
Phil Miller
Paul Miller (via Pete)
Sasi Milmo
Andrew Milner
Oliver Milton
Alex Minnis
Dr Paul Minton
Benjamin Mitchell
Jim Mitchell
John Mitchell
John Mitchinson
Benjamin Moag
Jon Moakes
Dan Moat
Adrian Mogg
Gregoire Moinet
Chris Monahan
Puneeta Mongia
Martin Montford
Ben Moore
Chris Moore
Christopher Moore
Daniel Moore
David Moore
Dave Moores
Jade Moores
Jack Moran
Joanna Morgan
Joe Morgan
Kev Morley
Vince Morley
Steve Morris
Craig Morrish
Glenn Morrison

Kirsty Mort
Jake Mortimer
John Morwood
Julia Mosedale
Linda Moskowitz
Jurgen Mudveins
James Mulvany
Dave Mumblist
Mark Murdock
Alan Murphy
Mark Murphy
Ronan Murphy
Steven Murray
Heather Musgrave
Musk Up
Kevin Musson
Andrew Myers
James Nason
Carlo Navato
Matt Nelson
Katie Newell
Chris Newman
Jen Newton
Jonathan Ng
Natalie Nicholas
Steve Nicholls
Ben Nichols
Jeffrey Nichols
Helen & Andy Nicklin
Gillian Niven
Noggleboggleman
Daniel Nolan
Steven Norrie
Andy Northing
Jamie Norton
Sean Norwood
NRG IT Ltd
Dan O'Brien
Mark O'Connor
Shiv O'Connor
Paul O'Donovan
John O'Driscoll
James O'Gorman
Liam O'Keeffe
Mark O'Neill
Mark O'Neill
Edward Oaksford
Amy Ogden
Gramps Oldman
Mark Oliver
Marco Olmi
Anne Monrad Olsson
Johan Olsson
Bridget Orr
Martin Owen
Michael Owen
Andrew Palmer
Dan Palmer-Bancel
Jamie Pankhurst
Dave Pannell

Becki Park
Emma Parkinson
Huw Parkinson
Kieran Blake Parkinson
Jim Parsonage
Simon Partridge
Stephen Pascoe
Thomas Pateman
Alex Paterson
Kaz Patwa
Will Payton
Roger Peachey
David Peacock
Stewart Pearce
Luke Pearson
Neil Pearson
Andy Peel
Richard Pennock
Jon Penny
Chris Perkins
Andrew Perrett
Matt Perriss
Jane Perry
Deano Peters
Richard Peters
Gareth Phillips
Martin Phillips
Charles Pick
Thomas Pickard
Paweł Pieczul
Rob Pike
Steve Pike
James Pilcher
Olly Pilsworth
Jonathan Pinnock
Jon Place
Chris Platt
Dan Pledge
Logan van der Poel-Treacy
Justin Pollard
Jon Ponting
Linda Pooch
Daniel Pope
Derek Porter
James Porter
Richard Potter
Christopher Potts
Andrew Powell
Leigh Powell
John Power
Simon Pratt
Jon Preece
Carl Prescott
Alice Price
Gareth Priestley
William Prince
Christopher Prior
Fin Pritchard
Scott Pritchard
Alexander Prosser-Snelling

Edward Prosser-Snelling
Stephen The Lord Banon
  Punter
Joe Purdy
Gareth Quigley
Damien Quill
Rob Quincey
Daniel Rae
Nathan Rance
David Randles
Martyn Rankin
Chris Rawlinson
James Read
Tim Read-Lamb
James Reader
Guy Redshaw
Maxine Reeder
Simon Rees
Jack Reeves
Pete Reilly
Kevin Renskers
Zoe Revell
Catherine Reynolds
Carl Richards
Cy Richards
Mike Richards
Simon Richards
James Richardson
Jonathan Richardson
Kackers Richardson
Luke Richardson
Paul Richardson
Adam Riches
Phil Riches
Paul Riddlesworth
James Rider
Jonathan Ridge
David Alexander Riffkin
Jonnie Ritchie
rjek
Rob and Claire
Stuart Robb
Bryan Roberts
Darren Roberts
Esther Roberts
Iwan Roberts
John Henry Roberts
Kevin Roberts
Laura Roberts
Andy Robertson
Alex Robinson
John Robinson
Lea Robinson
Karen Robson
Michael Rochester
Paul Rodgers
Natalie Roe
Iain Rogers
Klaas Roggeman
Ashley Rolfmore

Malcolm Rose
Rosie Nick and Dave
Michael Ross
Morgan Ross
Sharon Rossiter
Gareth Rothon
Gemma Rowley
Andrew Rubotham
Jon Rumsey
Gerard Ryan
Peter and Hannah Ryan
Adam Ryder
Benjamin Ryder
Ste Rye
Archie Sample
Andrew Sanders
Louise Sarjeant
Michael Sauer
David & Paul Savage
Mike Savill
Ian Sawyer
Peter Sayce
Adam Schofield
Jonathan Schwartz
George Scorey
Mich Scott
Raymond Scott
Henry Seal
Andrew Seaman
James Seamark
Jason Seddon
Oli Seddon
Scott Seiver
Mark Semmens
Dan Shanta
Laurence Shapiro
Jacob Sharlot
Daniel Sharp
Roger Sharp
Sam Sharp
John Sharp-Paul
Leigh Sharples
Scott Sharratt
Cameron Shaw
Daniel Shaw
Matt Sheehan
Andy Sheel
Andrew Sheldrick
Daniel Shepherd
James Shepherd
Jordan Shepherd
Giles Sheppard
Paul Sheridan
Darren Sherlock
Jim Shine
Jamie Shovelton
Kathryn Sidgwick
Jamie Simmonds
Kirsty Simms
Jonathan Simpson

Balvinder Singhru
Joe Skade
Jon Skeet
Simon Skelley
James Skinner
Matt Skinner
Wij Skinner
Dave Skywalker & Shazza
Iain Slack
Dan Slater
Natalie Slow
Edward Small
Chris Smart
Aaron Smith
Adam Smith
Alex Smith
Jess Smith
Jim Smith
Mark Smith
Matt Smith
Nathan Smith
Oli Smith
Rachel Smith
Richard Smith
Shaun Smith
Simon Smith
Steve Smith
Trevor Smith
Stuart Smith-Galer
Adam Smy
Carley Snow
Matthew Snowden
Sophie and Simon
Jack Sowerby
Seth Sowerby
Clare Sparks
Richard Sparks
Robin Spedding
Andrew Speers
Daniel Spence
Phil K Spencer
Jeremy Spolander
Philip Spyropoulos
David Stabeler
Neil Stabeler
Paul Stabeler
Jon Stace
Chad Stacey
Dean Stacey
Christopher J Stalker
Tom Stanford
Lydia Staniaszek
Andy & Liz Stanmore
Jay Stansfield
Jaine Stanway
Ian Stapleton
Lisa "Stuks" Staunton
Simon Staveley
Adrian Steel
Ben Steel

Derek Steele
Nigel and Lisa Steggel
Alistair Stevens
Linda Stevens
Toby Stevens
Chris Stevenson
Craig Stewart
Lauren Stimpson
Liam Stirk
Mike Stirrup
James Stone
Joel Stupple
Matthew Sturman
Carley Sullivan
Pauly & Sarah Surridge
Chris Suslowicz
Steve Sutherland
Marcus Sweeney-Bird
Swerni
Wayne Swithenbank
Jameel Syed
Mark Sykes
Nik Tabberer
Sarah Taft
Steve Tait
Symon Tait
Darren Talbot
John Talbot
Zak Talbot
Nick Tandy
Lee Tango
Nick Tanner
Paul Tarpey
Glenn Tate
Gordon Taylor
Ian Taylor
Jordan Taylor
Kate Taylor
Leonie Taylor
Lorna Taylor
Matt Taylor
Anthony Telford
Kevin Temple
Mark Temple
Ben Thacker
Tim Thacker
Callum Thomas
Guy Thomas
Barry Thomas-Brown
Liam Thompson
Stuart Thompson
Scott Thomson
Jared Thormahlen
Luke Thornley
Dave Thorp
Thomas Robert James
Tillings
Louise Timms
Craig Tims
Matthew Tinnelly

Ben Titmarsh
James Tobin
Alice Todd
Sam Tomlinson
Jennifer Tonner
Jonathan Tonner
Eoin Toomey
Paul Robert Thomas Toop
Darren Towler
Adrian Trangmar
Karl Travers & Vanessa
    Dalton
Alex Treadwell
Billy Trigg
Daniel Troll
James Tucker
Shane Tucker
Joel Tunbridge
Dan Turner
Ross Turner
Susie Tyler
Lewis Tyrrell
Andrew Unitt
Rod Upton
Andrew Urbanski
David Urquhart
Scott van Slyck
Kevin van Straelen
Kate Varlow
Gareth Vaughan
Michaela Veale
Ciaran Vinaccia
Nick Vincent
Paul Vincent
Violet and Joe
James Voce
Gabriel Vogt
Alex Vukmirovic
Christian Wacker
Emma Waight
Chris Wakefield
Martyn Wakefield
Tom Wakeling
John C.C. Walden
Andy Walker
Jonathan Walker
Mick Walker
Sam Walker
Susan Walker
Adam Wall
Alex Wall
Dominic Wall
Jack Wallace
Andrew Walmsley
Rachel Walmsley
Laura Walsh
Vic Walsh
Jeremy Walt
Adam Walton
Christopher Walton

David Walton
Paul Walton
Tim Wang
Aaron Ward
Andrew Ward
Dave Ward
Gary Ward
Jennifer Ward
Robert Ward
David Warner
Melvin Warner
Stuart Warner
James Warren
John Warren
Dan Warriner
Dave Watkins
Jade Watkins
Lizzy Watkins
Mark Watkins
Andrew Watson
Thomas Watson
Michael Watt
Chris Watts
Isabel Watts
Chris Webb
Daniel Webb
Dean Webb
Paul Webb
Terry Webb
Calum Weir
Kate Weir
Paul Weisel
James Wentworth-Bowyer
David Weston
Graeme Wharton
Hugo Wharton
Simon Wheadon
Ben Wheeldon
Paul Whelan
Angela While
Matthew Whitbourne
Nick Whitby
Pete Whitby
Martin White
Aiden Whitfield
Kerry Whittleton
Shane Whybrow
Andreas Wie
Damien Wildgoose
Louis Wilkerson-Roe
Phil Wilkinson
Jonathan Will
James Willcock
James Willetts
Christopher J. Williams
Mark Williams
Matt Williams
Matthew Williams
Steve Williams
Tom Williams

Peter Williamson
Isaac Willis
Gareth Wills
Chantelle Wilson
Craig Wilson
Danielle Wilson
Gareth Wilson
Martin Wilson
Pete Wilson
Richard Wilson
Stuart Wilson
John Windress
Malcolm Windsor
Dane Winterson
Sam Winthrop
Jason and Ann Wisnieski
Estelle Wolfers
Wonksie
Doris Woo
Alan Wood
Clare Wood
Ellie Wood
Ellis Wood
Paul Wood
Steve Wood
Thomas Wood
Michael Woodcock
Daniel Woodcraft
Ben Woodgate
Val Woodhouse
Stacey Woods
David Woolmer
Andrew Wootton
Lee Worgan
Alex Wright
Ben Wright
Jazelle Wright
Simon Yarwood
Gil Yeroslavsky
Harrison Yorke
Michael Yorke
Graham Young
Mark Young

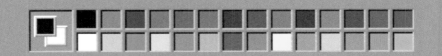